I am Success
WORKBOOK

BY
Ángela Quijada-Banks

Phase Illustrations by
Latika Peñarete

TABLE OF
CONTENTS

INTRODUCTION

As many of you know, more than 400,000 young people reside in foster care as of today and many of their parents' rights end up terminated. This brings us to the question, " What happens to the young people who age-out of foster care?" When publishing The Black Foster Youth Handbook, I had this in mind for the supportive adults who young people rely on to keep them safe, healthy, to a state of self sufficiency and interdependence. Through the 50+ Lessons , fostering success tips and #IAMSUCCESS Questions young people and supportive adults are able to dream big, identify goals and create a plan in order to achieve your wildest dreams! This workbook is to be supportive in the pursuit of what is understood in The Black Foster Youth Handbook as Soulful Liberation!

1.Root

- To help you and your adult supporter(s) gain understanding of some of the basics of foster care, and how you can begin to understand everyone's role and who to contact when your needs are not being met. After you gain that understanding, we kick off with grooming your mind to prepare you for the remaining chapters of this book.

2.Envision

- To help you and your supportive adult(s) understand the importance of working together. You will learn why you need healthy loving relationships around you and how to begin acquiring them.

3.Ascension

- Each chapter in this phase helps you build your self-confidence and further root and envision your life far beyond foster care. This phase will support you and your supportive adults' understanding of the next steps, and help you begin to actively seek out what you need in order to ensure your success.

4. Liberation

- In this last phase of this book, you will have understood the foundations of where you are in your life and where you want to go. You will have begun putting systems in place to support your big vision. You will know who you need in your life, and who you will need to release in order to achieve your version of success. You will also begin to uncover your divine purpose, do what is needed to achieve freedom from your past, and accelerate into soulful liberation.

THE R.E.A.L SUCCESS MODEL

PHASE 1
ROOT

Analyzing what you are currently rooted in. Assessing what may need to shift in order for different results. Recognizing what your current systems, routines and every day duties are.

Being clear on who are the current people in your life- are they bringing you quality support, authentic love and or guidance or is it time to shed some dead weight?

*Does the soil need to be changed? Do the roots need more water?**

PHASE 2
ENVISION

"What would life look like outside of the bubble I've placed for myself?"

How do I want to move forward despite my past trauma and pain to a vision bigger than what I previously accepted?

Dream big, don't concern too much on being "realistic".

Being focused on building your success team and identifying healthy relationships in your iiner circle.

What am I growing into?

PHASE 3
ASCENSION

Take it a step forward and identify the people who can help you realize your goals and dreams. Write your goals, the skills and habits needed to achieve your wildest dreams.

Begin to look at what is the legacy you wish to realize for your life.

**What am I choosing to water?? Who do I choose to become and how am I showing up in this way? **

> " Whether you believe you can or believe you can't, you're right. "

PHASE 4
LIBERATION

Liberating self (system) into defining a clear divine purpose, striving in awareness toward holistic health, growing community of success team players and giving back to communities we come from.

What is the quality of the fruit that I (or the system) is baring?

Liberation

Ascension

Envision

Root

The Black Foster Youth Handbook, Ángela Quijada-Banks ©2021

At the end of the day, these 4 R.E.A.L success phases can only support you in your journey if you are open to it, and ready to do the work. Nothing in this life worth acquiring will be "easy", at least not at first. Sometimes, when learning something new or starting a new habit, it can feel overwhelming until you get into the flow of your new reality. The best part about a new paradigm shift is you actually get to choose. You get to choose if you'd like to hold on to your limitations. You get to choose if you will make it a priority to heal and release generational curses from your family's lineage. You get to choose if you are ready and willing to achieve holistic healing and R.E.A.L success. Keep in mind that with every choice there are consequences and rewards. Choose wisely.

This model illustrates the inspired Maslow's Hierarchy of Needs tri- angle expanded with African and Indigenous spiritual systems and the representation of a "being" or "system". This is a visual representation of how this book is taking you from Root to Soulful Liberation. Before you begin your journey, take a moment and send an email to info@soulfulliberation.com with the SUBJECT LINE : " I AM COMMITTED TO SOULFUL LIBERATION! " The truth is we are more likely to follow through with our commitments if we 1. Write it down and 2. Tell at least one friend See you on the other side !

ROOT
phase one

Chapter 1:

THE BASICS TO UNDERSTANDING THIS NEW REALITY

- What does foster care mean to you in your words?

- What type of foster care placement are you in?

- When there is something that goes on regarding my foster parent who can I contact?

★ Rights in Foster care

- Foster care • Kinship care • 400,000• 250,00 • Siblings bill of rights
- Foster/resource parent • Case manager / Social worker • GAL/casa
- Independent living coordinators • Links • Independent living programs
- Foster youth bill of rights

1. Programs help to develop skills to young people in foster care without the presence of foster care officials

2. All of the things you have rights to do and not to do.

3. They are appointed judges to advocate on behalf of foster care child.

4. Coordinators help to support youth in foster care's transition into adulthood.

5. Independent living programs in North Carolina name one.

6. Is a temporary placement of a person or people with the intent of reunification with the biological family.

7. Childrens and youth were placed with family members Initially

8. Foster youth in the US alone

9. Children are placed into the foster care system in the US annually.

10. It will help siblings advocate or eachother.

11. An adult to support and help you navigate life and foster care.

12. Mandated reporters which means they have to report anything that is illegal or a harm to you and others.

★ True or False

1. Foster parents must be licensed by a foster care agency or the department of social services.
2. Foster parents are paid to take the child in.
3. It's okay for foster parents to not be financially stable to have a foster care child at their home.
4. Independent living programs are programs usually geared at youth thirteen to twenty one years old.
5. Health care for youth in foster care is available until 40 years old.

What type of placement are you in?

- LIST EMERGENCY CONTACTS HERE:

I AM SUCCESS WORKBOOK

Fostering Success

Scavenger Hunt

Name of players:

Have a tour of new place	Knows Home rules	Knows when and how to access food/water	Has signed Agreement of responsibilities	Has created a Vision board for the year
Has completed the 21 day mind challenge	Is on track with school studies	Has found their ideal therapist and is going regualarly	has created a resting routine they absolutely love	Knows the status of their case plan
Has begun researching scholarships and grants for post-secondary education	Has created a mind map of their ideas	Has been writing in their journal for over 60 days	has had 3 really hard days but decided each time to make it a good one	Has been learning more about how to take care of their hair
Knows the role of the CASA/GAL	Has created a rising routine that gives them energy	has been drinking atleast 5 glasses of water daily	Has shut their negative self talk up with positive self talk	Knows the role of their social worker
has been taking steps to strengthen their spirituality	has ten people they deem as part of their success team	has uncovered their divine purpose in this life	has tried something new that they enjoy	knows the role of their foster parent
has been taking steps to love themselves just as they are	knows what to do and who to call when they do not feel safe	has been challenging themselves to do things outside of their comfort zone	has spoken up about something that bothers them	knows all of their foster youth bill of rights

Chapter 2

REDEFINING YOU

- After reading through chapter one, I'm sure you have tons of questions. Think for a moment then write them in the space below. You can come back to them whenever you'd like. Some of your questions and thoughts may even prepare you for your next meeting with your social worker.

Lesson 1:
PRIORITIZING A RELATIONSHIP WITH YOURSELF

WHAT IS THE FIRST STEP IN REDEFINING YOUR-SELF?

#Self-Reflection:

Results from the 16 personalities test at **www.16personalities.com**:

Lesson 2:
LIVE IN THE MOMENT AND CAPTURE THE MEMORIES

Which can you focus on doing more?(circle two you'd like to focus on now)

a. Become more conscious of your physical breathing.
b. Practice gratitude.
c. Notice what you do not like, and begin to brain- storm how you can improve or change it.
d. Engage all of your senses with intention and relaxation.
e. What memories are we choosing to relive?

Why?

I AM SUCCESS WORKBOOK

Lesson 3:
BEING ACCOUNTABLE FOR YOUR ACTIONS

- What is something that has happened to me in the past that I believe will hold me back from being successful in the future?
- What do I believe could come up and be in the way of my happiness in the future?
- What can I do to minimize my exposure to or completely eliminate this blockage?
- If I had three wishes to use on my path toward success, what would they be?

Lesson 4:
TRAUMA DOESN'T DEFINE MY FUTURE

Below is an article I wrote when I was 21. The beginning was changed when it was published, which caused some inconsistency with- in it's message. However, this is the original text. I was asked, "What does resilience mean to you?"

Resilience, to me, is the constant quick bounce-back to the best ability of a being regardless of any or every situation that exerts a significant amount of physical, mental, emotional and/or spiritual stress.

Some of us are born with resilience and others can learn it. There are some that have a genetic connection to it followed by the constant experience that life gives them to continue to exercise the craft.

I'm not quite sure if I was born with it, but I do know that I have it. There are many ways to harness and master the art. One way to un- derstand more about resilience is to find out what your ACE Score is.

What Are ACES?

An ACE assessment is a test that measures an individual's Adverse Childhood Experiences. After taking the assessment, which ranges from scores of 1-10, you will be able to understand yourself more in depth and see which coping skills work best to heal in all areas. Personally, I had resilience long before taking the ACE assessment, however, it helped me to understand myself better and why I would be or act a certain way towards others or specific situations.

As a former foster youth, my ACE score ended up being a 9/10 which was alarming at first, however, you must remember that information is inherently a good thing. It's what you do with that information that counts. How can you address something if you have no idea it exists? It's kind of like being oblivious in a toxic relationship. You have no idea what a healthy blueprint of a relationship looks like so you just endure the high toxicity until you find out on a show, with a friend or on the internet that being yelled at

and passively aggressively shoved etc is not a conducive relationship. With that information, you are able to then seek assistance. In the case of this scenario, couples counseling or learning how to effectively communicate would be helpful in the solutions. This leads to the next extremely significant way one can build resilience: being honest with yourself. In different situations, it may be hard to understand or accept the reality of your current situation. As a youth who has experienced several adverse childhood traumas before, during and post foster care, I can say that it was difficult ,at first, to fully acknowledge all of the events that led up to who I am today.

It's important to be honest with yourself every step of the way. You have to really understand who you are and what makes you upset, angry, frustrated, excited, joyous, ecstatic etc. It matters because after you recognize and understand this then you can heal.

Being resilient means being patient with yourself, persisting even if you don't get something right the first time or second...or third, and to persevere through all obstacles.

Find your purpose. Look deep within and ask yourself who or what is your motivation? What's keeping you going or who are you doing it for? Remember to always take care of yourself. Self-care is one of the most undermined qualities anyone and everyone should learn to obtain.

Things like yoga, reading a book, poetry, meditation, taking deep breaths and creating a garden are a few hobbies that can get your mind off of everything for a few moments. This will help you reassess what or how you're thinking about something and help you build resilience!

Now, get out there warriors and start perfecting the art of your own resilience!

Resilience is me. Resilience is YOU. Resilience is us.

This article was published and distributed to all 100 counties in North Carolina.

#IAMSUCCESS QUESTIONS

- What does resilience mean to you?
- When was the first time you had to be resilient?
- What other tools can you add into your Toolbox when life gets hard again?
- What ways can you begin to be aware of your inner child and nurturing that side of you?
- What have you been avoiding that needs your attention?

Lesson 5:
THE IMPORTANCE OF A RISING AND RESTING ROUTINE

SUMMER 2019 MY RISING WAS:

5:00 am - Awaken and Shower (with chanting / listening to Affirmations)
5:15 am - Wash my face/ brush my teeth in robe
5:30 am - Light Work out/ yoga w/ motivational speech or podcast
5:45 am - Meditation and journal insight, intentions, and gratitude for the day
6:15 am - Talk to my fiancé who was in Japan
6:30 am - Make up and get dressed while listening to hype music
6:50 am - Drink 3 glasses of warm water with lemon
7:00 am - Be ready for the day ahead

What is your ideal rising routine?

What is your ideal resting routine?

I AM SUCCESS WORKBOOK

(PREVIOUS MONTH)

- Describe the previous month in three words
  Example: July was... Electric, different, stressful.
- What were the best moments of the previous month that you always want to remember?
- What was one lesson you learned this previous month?
- What is one thing you are proud of from this month?
- What is one thing that you did not like that happened this month and how will you improve this in the future?

(NEW MONTH)

- Set your intentions for this new month in three words or less.
  Example: August is vibrant and exciting!
- What are your top 3 goals that you want to accomplish in this month?
- How do you want to feel this month?
- What will you put into place this month from what you have
- learned in the previous month?
  Example: In the previous month, I learned that I need to learn how to set strong boundaries between my friends and myself. I will be asking others how to do this, reading books, and watching YouTube videos on how to effectively protect my space so that what happened last month does not happen again.

Lesson 6:
BLACK HISTORY IS STILL RELEVANT TODAY

- What comes to mind when you think of Black history?
- What do you think about when you think back to slavery?
- How is black and Indigenous history depicted in your school?
- What amazing things are you currently doing to support your community?
- What amazing things would you like to do to support your community?
- How can you begin to learn more about your ancestry?

Chapter Exercise
DIGITIZING MEMORIES AND ACCOMPLISHMENTS

Sometimes, due to back-to-back trauma, we forget who we are. I did. We are much more than cool titles, job positions, material possessions, and the accomplishments we acquire; however, that doesn't mean they don't matter. They just don't matter as much in comparison to our core values, the quality of relationships we keep, and our purpose in this life. Memories and accomplishments help us root in ourselves and build self-confidence.

Digitize your memories and accomplishments so if you have to move, you will have them with you. I left multiple items in the different foster homes I was in and unfortunately, I did not get them back.

Google photos is a free resource you can use to upload photos to the google photos drive. Another thing that you can do is Archive photos on Instagram or Facebook.

Honestly, the end of 2019 is really when I recognized I had a problem with completely forgetting who I was and the accomplishments I had. Why? Well, because I was used to being in survival mode all of the time. After recognizing this, I hopped on the phone to speak with my mentor Dr. Regina Williams. She suggested I create a Brag Board. I thought the concept was incredible! I had never thought about creating something to help me remember what I accomplished over the years. I didn't know what I would want to put on a poster board, but I would create something none the less because forgetting what i'd done

in the past was an ongoing problem. After some thought and a few days passing, I made a decision to create an online portfolio to remind me of some of the most reputable accomplishments I fortunately got photographed.

(www.originalsoulflower.com under "who is she")

You do not have to create an entire website like I did, but you may want to create something that helps remind you of the amazing accomplishments you have completed thus far and in the future.

It could be a poster board, as she suggested, or it can be a private Facebook album where you document your fun, loving memories and celebrations that perhaps only you want to see. Maybe it is a private Instagram account where you document your weight loss journey.

I send photos and videos to myself all the time, and the portfolio keeps getting bigger!

Another idea is to create a hidden google photos album and only add people to it that you know will encourage a great business or college venture along the way!

But take awareness of yourself and your current ability to assess your accomplishments while documenting and savoring beautiful moments of the process.

Speaking of which, excuse me while I go revamp my online portfolio

- **Who am I**
- **Accomplishments**

RIMY MORRIS

"If you are currently experiencing foster care, I want you to know that right now it seems like it'll never end but it does. As you get to know yourself, I hope you never limit yourself like foster care does. You can be both strong and vulnerable. You can be kind and firm. You can be as big or as small as you need to be. There is a duality to you and it is BEAUTIFUL. I hope that you show up as your full self in this world because you deserve that. I'm rooting for you always."

After spending 11 years in care, I aged out. I left foster care knowing very little about myself or the world I was being sent out into. I didn't have a plan for becoming a young adult, in fact, I didn't even think I would be alive to see life after foster care. I am so grateful that I am. When I aged out, I didn't have a person to help me figure it out. I searched for purpose alone with no guidance. I made many mistakes but allowed myself grace every time. As I got to know me and the world around me, I was able to find places where I fit and was appreciated. I found people who cared for me and slowly I saw things start to align for me. I stayed true to myself no matter what and I was blessed with opportunities that I couldn't have ever dreamt of. I have done things that I still I can't believe it sometimes. I have gotten to work with congress, started a business-Raising Resilience, won a national award, wrote and illustrated 2 workbooks for foster parents, and am a paid employee with a service provider that used to service me while I was in care.

There are so many big things that I'm proud of but the things that bring me the most joy are the small things. I bought my first car in cash, can afford to live comfortably in a place alone, and have an amazing best friend who loves me and supports me. So many things have changed but the biggest thing is me. I learned to treat myself like I like me. I used to search for love and validation from the world but realized that I can give myself everything I was seeking.

I learned that I deserve good things contrary to what others had convinced me of when I was younger. The truth is, the healthiest love that ever gotten to partake in is with myself. It was the one thing that changed everything for me. Outside of learning to love myself, I wish I would've had a tool to help me on this journey when I was younger. I could've really benefited from "The Black Foster Youth Handbook".

I truly believe that "The Black Foster Youth Handbook" is one of the most amazing tools for young people in care because the best advice comes from people who have done it before you. Many of us went into the world with no idea what we were doing and "got it out the mud". Now we can pass down these lessons and tips to the next generation so that they don't have to make the same mistakes we made. They're not doing it alone. I want to provide tools to give more of us a chance at success.

Learn more about Rimy & Raising resilience at www.soulfulliberation.com/resources

Chapter 3

THE MINDSET TO SUCCESS

Lesson 7:

YOU DO NOT HAVE TO DO IT ALONE

#IAMSUCCESS QUESTIONS:

- Have you ever felt alone?
- Do you believe that you do not need anyone?
- What is the importance of having healthy-minded people in your circle?
- Say, "I do not have to do life on my own. There are people who care about me. There are people who will support me. I am not alone." Choose one word to describe how saying the above statement makes you feel.
- Write one word to describe how you feel right now.

Lesson 8:
EVERYTHING IS TEMPORARY!

- Who are you today, and who will you be?
- What did you learn from the negative situations that happened to you?
- What can you do to change your current life outcomes?

Lesson 9:
YOU CAN DEFINE WHAT SUCCESS IS FOR YOURSELF

#IAMSUCCESS QUESTIONS:

- Which of the 7 P's of success stood out to you the most? Why?
- What type of shows/music/movies or social media posts do you feed your mind with? On a scale of 1-5 (5 being the most patient), how patient are you?
- How do you define success?

Lesson 10:

CHECK YO' SELF BEFORE YOU WRECK YOURSELF

Two Different Mindsets:

1. Abundance

- I can earn all the money I want
- Maybe I don't know how but I will find a way
- How can I afford that?
- There's a lot of possibilities out there
- All I have to do is learn and I will apply the rest
- I'm going to start reading financial literacy books or watching financial education videos on YouTube.

2. Scarcity

- Broke as hell, help me
- I wish I could afford that
- I am not going to make it
- There's no hope for me
- This is just the cards I was dealt
- I don't know how to start so I guess it's not for me
- Which one sounds more like you? Number 1 or Number 2?
- Has anyone ever told you that money was the root of all evil?

- ○ What is the first step you will take to ensure you begin learning financial literacy?
- ○ Why is becoming financially literate so important?
- ○ What would you do if you made the money you desired?

Lesson 11:

EMOTIONS ARE ENERGY IN MOTION.

- What is the true definition of EMOTION?
- Which emotion comes up for you when someone or something upsets you?
- Why is it important for you to cultivate this energy in motion?
- How will you use that energy into something constructive moving forward?
- What are some ways you can share this energy in motion with the people you love and care about?
- What is your favorite genre of music? Why?
- How often do you listen to music?
- Name a time that you felt called to speak up and you didn't.
- Name a time you said something and you wish you didn't. Why? What happened?
- Think back to the first time you danced. How did you feel?
- What can you do today to connect with your emotions in a healthy way?

Lesson 12:

DREAM BIG, NO BIGGER !

Chapter Exercise
HOW TO START AND FINISH THE NO NEGATIVE SELF-TALK
72 HOUR CHALLENGE.

For three days (72) hours, you will refrain from talking negatively about yourself and others.

You will unfollow / unfriend/ block any pages on social media that do not contribute to the person you are becoming. You will not make excuses for why you need any form of toxicity.

You will write in your journal or say out loud, something or someone that you love whenever a negative thought comes up. You will focus on
harnessing and creating new happier moments.

To help you stay focused, write down affirmations or positive, uplifting quotes from people you respect and admire. Put them all over
your space. Put them on your laptop screen. Make some of them your phone screen saver. So that way, when your mind starts drifting you
can find encouragement in as many spaces as you can.

Go back through your rising routine and be sure when you are waking up that you are taking control of your day. Declare that you will not allow that negative voice to win.

One thing that helped me when I was starting out was giving this negative voice an image... an image that made me laugh.

For instance, when that negative voice with limiting beliefs would come up I'd envision it being a kissy face emoji. The voice isn't so scary
as a kissy face emoji. Then I gave it a different voice. A squeaker voice. And now it's a kissy face emoji with a squeaker voice. How hilarious!

After envisioning this in my mind, I would move this hilarious image to be right in front of me. I'd laugh at it as I lower the voice into a whisper.

Then I would minimize the gigantic kissy face emoji to fit in the palm of my hand. I really would have fun with it. I threw it on the floor and stomped on it. No more negative voices.

If you recognize your negative self-talk is coming up more and more, that's okay. It's all a part of the process! You just have to stick with it.
Maybe start off with a 24 hour challenge and then slowly move up to a 72 hour, a 7 day, a 14 day, a 21 day until this becomes second nature
for you! Remember, this is not about who gets it done faster or the best. It's about your own individual progress in taking control of your mind and your own internal conversations. You got this!

For my high achievers, here is a Streak tracker for a no negative self-talk for 21-28 days challenge! Be sure to establish what you will be doing for this 21 day challenge, why it is important that you do it and the reward you will receive once you complete it!

I AM SUCCESS WORKBOOK

VICTOR SIMS

When I think about youth who are currently experiencing foster care I believe that the best thing that I can tell them is to find hope. Find an opportunity to see the world differently. We all have a hard game of cards to place sometimes we just have to find out when to put out the cards we have out and when is the best opportunity to play the game, who do we play the game with and who don't we play it with. I used to tell my children that the best thing that we can do is think about the way that people talk about us and try to change it. More tangible advice would be to change the way that we all see ourselves.

I grew up in Florida's foster care system without the stability of a permanent home and supportive family for 11 years prior to being adopted. From my work helping to improve children's experiences when they are removed from their parents to my TEDx Talk on the importance of social capital for youth in care, I have focused on bringing about positive changes to the foster care system. I helped SailFuture to pilot an innovative case management program for teenagers who were sleeping in offices. I reduced the amount of children sleeping in offices by 100% within 4 months by creating partnerships and building capacity for those caring for children in foster care through recruitment of kinship families.

I travel throughout Florida and the country speaking to legislators about creating reform for youth in care. I have advocated for a bill of rights for children in foster care as well as efforts to ensure that every child has a plan for permanency. In addition to serving on the National Foster Youth and Alumni Policy Council, I have met with legislators in support of the Family First Prevention Services Act. In June 2019,I was recognized by the American Bar Association as a Reunification Hero. I share my experiences to ensure that children have a chance for reunification and beyond. I was recognized as a 2020 Casey Excellence for Children Award as an Alumni in care. In 2021 I was recognized from the Treehouse Foundation as part of their Re-Envisioning Foster Care in America Champion.

In 2020 I founded a Non-Profit Organization called Guiding Hope. The Non-Profit organization focuses on mentorship and building relationships with children in Foster Care who identify as LGBTQ by creating safe havens within the system of care where they are recognized for who they are, reducing high risk behaviors by 82% such as self-harm, sexual activity, substance misuse and truancy.

Learn more about Victor & Guiding Hope at www.soulfulliberation.com/resources

ENVISION
phase two

Chapter 4:

EVOLVING DEFINITIONS

Lesson 13:

HOME IS NOT JUST A FIXED DESTINATION

#IAMSUCCESS QUESTIONS:

- What comes to mind when you think of the word, "home"?
- How do you define a home?
- What could you or your supportive adult do now, to make you feel more at home?
- How would you like to redefine home for yourself?
- Home is (fill in the blank)

Lesson 14:
NOT EVERYONE IS YOUR ENEMY

- Have you ever had someone mistreat you?
- What is your definition of trust?
- How do you show others that you trust them?
- How can you tell if someone is trustworthy?
- Do you gossip with others?
- What is one thing you can do to replace gossiping?

Lesson 15:
SETTING BOUNDARIES IS AN ACT OF SELF-LOVE

#IAMSUCCESS QUESTIONS:

- Why is it important to have boundaries?
- Does everyone in your inner circle honor what you think and say?
- How do they show that they honor you?
- Do you feel like you may be walking on eggshells with certain people?

Lesson 16:
BLOOD ISN'T ALWAYS THICKER THAN WATER.

- What can you do when you need extra support?
- Who do you trust the most in your circle right now? Why?
- What is the importance of your supportive adult (s) in your circle? How can you begin to better get to know your supportive adult(s)? Why is it important that you get to know them better?

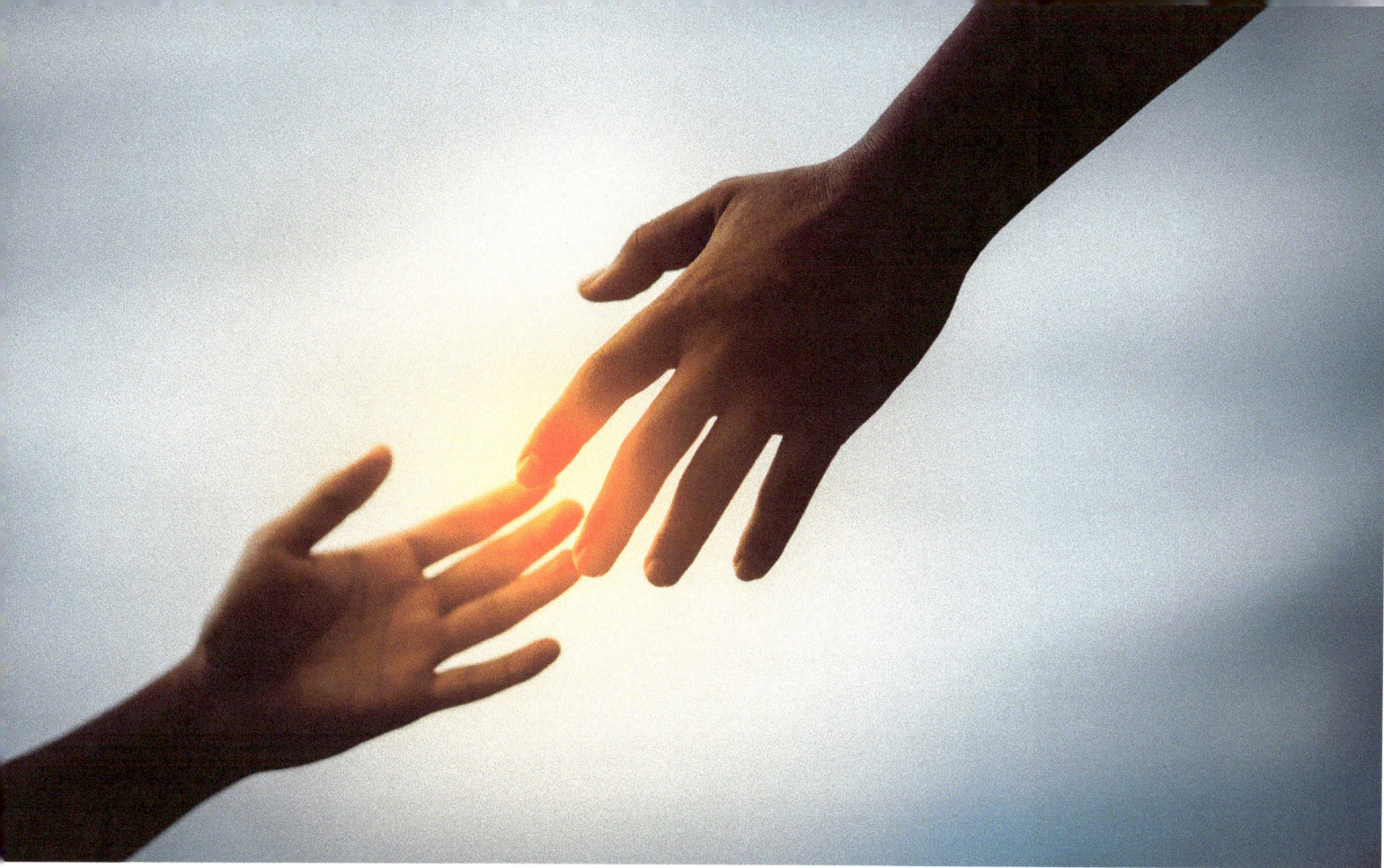

Lesson 17:

RELATIONSHIPS ARE PIVOTAL TO YOUR SUCCESS

SKETCH YOUR MESS

You will need:

- 2-4 sheets of paper
- Something to sketch with
- colored pens/crayons/ markers to add details
- Minimum of 30 minutes of spare time
- You may do this alone, with other young people or with a supportive adult

Set a timer for 10 minutes. First sketch the person that you have known yourself to be. The sketch does not have to be perfect. You don't have to be extremely artistic to complete this exercise. Be detailed in your perception of yourself. Add descriptions to your sketch to label your hair, your lips, your body, your clothing and your personality. Now, sketch two people that are always around you. How do they look? How do you perceive their personalities to be? Make sure to use captions and descriptive words to bring clarity to your sketch. Take your time and use all of the time allotted to be detailed in your sketch. After the timer has run out, take a step back and look at your sketch.

Now, set your timer for another 10 minutes. This time, on a separate piece of paper draw yourself with the physical and personality characteristics you wish to embody. Maybe you are smiling in this picture and your hair is done up a certain way. Maybe you are holding a book, like this one ;) to remind you that you would like to be a reader. Maybe you sketch yourself outside, meditating because that is something you want to begin adopting into your habits. Wonderful, now that you have sketched your ideal self- it is time to sketch who an ideal supportive adult would look and act like. Take a moment to think this through. Do not rush the process. Think of the physical and personality characteristics you would want two supportive adults to embody. What do they look like? How would they act toward you? What is it feel like to be around them? (Btw: "I don't know" is not an acceptable answer.)

VERONICA KRUPNIC

"To the children and youth, whose lives have been touched by the system, I would like to share the words I wish someone had shared with me. You and the wisdom from your experiences are enough, do not let anyone tell you or make you feel otherwise. I have spent far too much of my life and energy compromising myself, my values and experiences to make others feel comfortable or to appease them, which was only detrimental to myself and my own light.

I would also share that one of the most influential parts of my journey to healing has been finding what makes my soul happy. For me, this was through reconnection to what I like to call my generational joy. By generational joy, I mean the strong and undeniable sense of belonging or home, which I found in the connection to my indigenous roots. Another source of connection and belonging, I never thought I'd end up leaning on, has been the foster alumni community. Home is not always a location but often a feeling, and I'm grateful I've found that feeling within this community. Lastly, I will say remain true to yourself, your experience and values by showing up imperfectly human, authentically and passionately. Know that you are in the driver's seat; your life, your future and your healing are defined by you."

My name is Veronica Krupnick and I am proudly Indigenous, a member of the Hopi Tribe of Arizona with Jemez Pueblo and Navajo heritage. I graduated with my bachelor's degree from Fort Lewis College in 2017 and am currently attending New Mexico Highlands University, pursuing a master of social work degree, the first in my biological family to do so. I have spent the last several years following my passion for supporting youth in foster care, and have established myself as a local, state and national leader within child welfare. In my role as the Mentorship, Advocacy and Peer Support (MAPS) Program Coordinator with CASA First, I am able to provide peer support for transitional aged youth in foster care and to provide authentic insight and lived experience perspective to service providers in the community. I am honored to be a part of a collective of powerful, young voices throughout the country fighting to transform the child welfare system every day. I am currently a member of the Child Welfare and Race Equity Collaborative, the New Mexico Partners, Tewa Women United and the National Foster Youth and Alumni Policy Council. My aspiration is to continue my journey to become a thriving, unapologetic, heart-led Indigenous Leader who supports the holistic well-being and healing journey of indigenous people and communities, as well as those who have been impacted by the foster care system.

During and after my time in foster care, I was constantly overwhelmed with frustration as I attempted to adjust to my new reality, while still feeling the heartbreak from my past and the uncertainty and fear of my future. I had begun to believe that there was something "wrong" with me because I was unable to simply "move on from the past". What I realized later in life was that there is no right time or way to begin to heal,
and this is a personal journey and not something that can or should be forced. It has taken me over a decade of failures, successes, healing and learning to figure out who I am, in my heart, and where I envision myself going, and even still my story is evolving.

Learn more about Veronica at www.soulfulliberation.com/resources

Chapter 5:

BUILDING YOUR SUCCESS TEAM

Lesson 18:

YOU MUST BE A GOOD FRIEND TO HAVE A GOODFRIEND

#IAMSUCCESS QUESTIONS:

- Are you a good friend? How do you know?
- What is the evidence to support that you are a good friend?
- How Can you be a better friend to others?
- Do you have good friends in your circle?
- What is one way that you like to show love to others?
- How would you like your friend to show love to you?

Lesson 19:
REAL LOVE IS NOT HARD TO IDENTIFY.

#IAMSUCCESS QUESTIONS:

- What does a "toxic relationship" look like?
- How many toxic relationships can you count in your life right now?
- How many toxic relationships are you in?
- What does a "healthy relationship" look like?
- How many healthy relationships can you create?
- How can you learn more about how to create and maintain more healthy relationships?

Lesson 20:
MARRIAGE IS STILL AN OPTION

- What have I learned from people in my circle?
- What do I value most from myself and others?
- Who are 3 people I trust and admire? Why?
- What have I learned from past interactions the hard way? What were the lessons?
- How can I be sure that I am not repeating the same mistakes in my relationships?

Lesson 21:
INTIMACY IS NOT JUST SEX

#IAMSUCCESS QUESTIONS:

- How do YOU define love?
- How do you express love?
- What do you know about sex (other than you or your partner needs to wear a condom)?
- What are ways that you can be intimate with someone without sex?
- What boundaries do you have for yourself when it comes to sex?
- Why is it important to have clear expectations of intimacy?
- What are your clear expectations when it comes to romantic relationships and sex?

Lesson 22:

HEALTHY RELATIONSHIPS ARE RECIPROCAL

- How can you work harmoniously with your foster/resource parent(s), social worker, and GAL?
- Make sure to be honest with yourself about your current relationships in your life.
- Ask yourself "Are they feeding my flame?" Yes or no. And how are they feeding my flame?

BUILD YOUR SUCCESS TEAM

Begin thinking about who you want to include in your success team.nThroughout your time in foster care, begin to develop a list of 10-15 trustworthy adults that agree to being in your life after foster care. If that seems overwhelming, start off with just one and go from there.

Establish what their relationship is to you and how you would like for them to support you. The adults are also able to establish how they will know that you are showing appreciation for their time, efforts and support.

Now use this sheet to actually contact them and meet up with them in person. Let them know you would like them to be on your success team.

I,_____have agreed to become a part of_____

_____'s success team. This means that I will_____

_____

_____

And when times get tough or I do not agree with a behavior, I will_____

_____

_____

_____

I, _____ am excited to have you on my success team. I will show my appreciation for our relationships by_____
_____
_____ *example: call you and update you on my progress every week/ month/ year
If i become frustrated with something you say or do, I will_____
_____
_____
_____
My current goals are:(You can say this verbally)_____
_____
_____
I would like to reach them by (give yourself a
date)_____
_____
Please hold me accountable for this by: _____
_____
_____
If I do not reach my goals of_____
_____
_____
Then_____
_____
_____(list consequence).

Together, we agree to voluntarily come together in a success circle and have a reciprocal nature of relationship so that I can continue to build myself up to become the best me that I can be.

* Adult supporter ** I am grateful that:

_____

_____

Young person * I am grateful to have you on my team because:

_____

_____

We sign this agreement to affirm all the above to be true and valid. Our signatures symbolize our commitment to each other's success and as a step closer to furthering the strength of our relationship.

_____(young person signature)

_____Adult signature)

FosterClub has this sheet, called Permanency Pact to help with establishing lasting relationships with people in the foster care system. It's imperative to know what each person is doing and how to support their work.

I am very much about reciprocal relationships and so I have expanded on that work to create a side where the adults are able to share how they would like to be supported as well. All relationships are a two-way street. Relationships in foster care are no different. This sheet will help you and your supportive adult(s) be clear on their roles and how they'd like to support you.

When a young person is expressing themselves, do not always feel like you have to agree with what they say. Challenge them and ask them why they think what they think. Allow them to dive deeper into their ideas and maybe come to a different conclusion on their own. This is not to be in a chastising or belittling way, more so an invitation to express clear thoughts, opinions, and ideas.

EMILIO SWANN

What is the point of surviving if you can't Live after? That's the question I carried with myself during my adult life after aging out of the Fostercare system. It may be a question you have as well.

I entered the system twice. The first, being only a toddler, I was stripped from my dysfunctional family and placed in a dysfunctional system. Separated from my siblings, derived from my culture, and had any sense of love, safety, and normalcy stripped from me. 7 houses in just 5 years but never a home. To this day I still don't know if it was an intervention for the better or for the worst. But I do know it put me through the first half of my journey.

The second time I entered the system was different. I was adopted at the age of 11, and although that sounds like a happy ending, it was anything but. Once again I faced the same abuse and neglect. Except this time it was from people I thought I could call family. I was put into life threatening situations time after time until eventually I decided to take action. Instead of being taken, I sought the system out for help. Being much older, I was able to advocate for myself and take more control of the decisions that would be made for my life. Which led to my path to aging out of the system and becoming an adult. The end of one chapter in my life and the beginning to the next. I know..I know that I skimmed through 18 years of my life in one paragraph. But it's no use sharing all the trauma in my childhood if it's not for an educational purpose.
Plus, surviving is the easy part. The hard part is living.

A soldier is a survivalist for a reason. After intense training and countless real life experiences, surviving becomes a second hand nature to them. But coming back from a drilled in lifestyle and adjusting back to the "normal" civilian way is near impossible to do. Similarly, as a former foster youth I faced the same obstacle. After all that trauma, after all the abuse and neglect, after all the life threatening situations, and to top it all off, face it as a child with no voice nor authority to make changes, surviving became a second hand nature to myself as well. But how do you turn a traumatizing backstory into an inspirational transformation of healing and success. To be able to maintain a good mental, social, and physical health. Hold down stable healthy relationships and set necessary boundaries. And create and pursue dreams to one day achieve whatever success means to you. Seems impossible right? Well, you're holding a book written by someone who has proven that even the impossible is possible. Someone I look up to for not letting their past become an excuse of why they can't but instead, an inspiration of why they will.

As for me, well… I'm currently on my path. Still defining who I am, who I will become, and what things I will achieve along the way. As a young man, I have many goals and dreams. But one stands out more than others. I call it the "Golden Dream". To be happy, mentally and emotionally stable, and physically healthy. Financially stable. Surrounded by friends and family who truly support me. And in an environment that continuously recharges me when I'm drained. But dreams require action. So here I am. Accomplishing one goal at a time.

At the moment, I am overwhelmed with the various paths I'm pursuing. Who said you could only have one dream? I turned a couple of my what were once just hobbies into small side businesses. Music Production, Fashion Design, Photography/Videography, and Motivational Speaking are just a few of many. At the same time holding down two jobs as a Kinship Caregiver licensing trainer and Photography studio coordinator. I plan to take all my interests and experiences and make businesses out of them. After I achieve all the dreams and goals it still doesn't stop. I will use my platform to create an organization that teaches former foster youth how to turn their hobbies and passions into businesses. Give them the opportunity to achieve success and live a life that may have once seemed impossible.

When it comes to the "Black Foster Youth Handbook"… Well lets rewind back to when I was just a kid without a voice. Continuously let down time after time by adults. Losing faith in them as well as value in myself. As I reflect on my childhood, I sometimes paint the picture of me as a kid driving a car with my window rolled up. Now of course this is my first time driving so I'm destined to run into obstacles. Flat tires, running out of gas, accidents, metaphorically of course. But you see the problem isn't the obstacles. It's the window that I have rolled up. Blocking anyone from getting in. From any advice reaching my ears. Any love from reaching my heart. No sense of where I'm going, just pressing the gas and hoping for the best. A child destined for failure.

Of Course I survived, however it was anything but easy. Scars that would stay with me the rest of my life. Hindered on my path to success because I had no sense of direction and ended up going the wrong way. It would have been so much easier if I had some help. Some advice. Someone. Imagine how much further I would be. If only I had a map. A map that showed me where I was, where I needed to be, and the best route to get there. Imagine I had an owners manual. So I could see just how to fix and heal my metaphorical vessel. Imagine I had a passenger. Someone who has been on the same path that I was on, in my corner for support. That is what "TBFYH" could have been for me.

So it serves no purpose to me now right? Wrong! See not only is the handbook a well written survivalist tool. It is also a start to a new path. I currently use it for self-reflection, Inspiration, and to practice self-healing. Those years I had spent surviving for so long stuck with me. They had become a part of me. Both good and bad experiences. Strengths along with the weaknesses. I have another difficult journey ahead of me with new obstacles and more challenges, but this time I have help. I will always be a survivalist. But now that I'm on a new path of life, I can live.

Learn more about Emilio at www.soulfulliberation.com/resources

Chapter 6:

MAINTAINING A CONNECTION TO YOUR CULTURE

Lesson 23:

BLACK PEOPLE WITH THE EXPERIENCE OF FOSTERCARE HAVE MADE IT BEFORE ME

#IAMSUCCESS QUESTIONS:

- How do you define your culture?
- What language(s) do you speak?
- What kind of food did you grow up eating?
- What are your top 3 favorite meals?
- Have you ever thought about your history? Do you resonate with Black history? Why or why not?
- What do you enjoy doing the most?
- What cultural identity do you identify with the most?
- Do you know the history of the ethnic group you come from?
- Do you have a desire to know this history? Why or why not?

Justin Hayden , Co-Founder of Raising Resilience

Lesson 24:

YOUR HAIR IS YOUR CROWN

Lesson 25:
GOING BACK TO YOUR ROOTS HELPS YOU MOVE FORWARD WITH CONFIDENCE AND CLARITY

#IAMSUCCESS QUESTIONS:

- Defining my culture now that I have been to so many homes
- What is my base?
- What do you enjoy celebrating?
- How do you identify yourself?
- What skill comes naturally to you?
- What do you enjoy doing the most?
- What are your thoughts on police brutality and mass incarceration?
- How does it make you feel when you watch the news?

Lesson 26:
FINDING A HEALTHY COMMUNITY IN YOUR CULTURE

Chapter Exercise
BUILDING YOUR CULTURAL CONNECTION THROUGH ART

Visit your nearest history and museums that showcase art and philosophies from Black and brown artists. Take lots of pictures and document
in your journal about what you've learned.

Look up cultural events that will help you navigate your cultural identity. Hang out with people that make you feel like you're at "home".
Be proactive in trying new ways of being and celebrating your culture. Let your supportive adult know what you are interested in doing. Even if they do not have the same ethnic background, invite them along!They might want to learn too!

Begin going to your local library to familiarize yourself with that environment. There are also free e-books all over the internet. Familiarize yourself with Black authors, your ethnicity of people's autobiographies,and stories that are uplifting and positive. Not just slave narratives.

Maybe even start a Book club!

Take a picture/ or draw something that depicts your historical roots and paste or tape it below
Be sure to include a title and caption so that you can refer back to it in the years to come!

MY READING GOALS

Year:
Name:

JANUARY	FEBRUARY	MARCH	APRIL	MAY	JUNE
JULY	AUGUST	SEPTEMBER	OCTOBER	NOVEMBER	DECEMBER

TAMISHA MACKLIN

"I want young people to know that there is hope lifewill get better; you will recover, so stay strong because you are resilient! The road to success is never easy and it takes a lot of hard work. What has helped me keep going over the years is setting goals and always planning for the future. I have learned many lessons along the way. Stay strong and always remember you can do anything you set your mind to! "

Hello My Name is Tamisha Macklin. I am 33 years old. I grew up in the child welfare system for many years ending up in the Juvenile Justice system, eventually aging out of care in 2007 at 19 years old.I love the work that I am blessed to doto walk alongside my youth to support them on their journey to Independence. It reminds me of my life story and the transition I had to get to where I am today. I am a Wife, Mother, and a College graduate. I work as a Housing Navigator, a Youth Program Manager, a Writer, and Poet.

My Foster care story started when my parents divorced when I was young. I had an older brother but we were separated at a very young age. He lived in California with my grandparents.

After the divorce my dad ended up gaining custody of me because of my mom's drug addiction to crack cocaine. By age six due to a dependency & neglect case against my dad I ended up in the child welfare system. During this time, I moved around between foster homes and family.

Eventually I ended up living with my grandparents until I completed elementary school. In Middle school, I moved back with my Dad. Even though the physical abuse stopped I continued to not be properly cared for. There were times that I wouldn't see my dad for weeks. I had no structure or boundaries in place. I needed parents to step up and properly raise me or even someone to just come in and check to see if I was ok. I also struggled with my mom's deteriorating health. She was in a coma due to a head injury she acquired when being pushed out of a moving car and was permanently disabled and needed long-term care.

Due to the lack of family support by the 6th grade at age 12, I thought I was grown. I was running the streets , hanging out with the wrong crowd, using drugs and alcohol, smoking cigarettes , not going to school, and getting in trouble with the law. Looking back I realized this was me crying out for help and seeking attention in a not so good way. I had extreme attachment issues.

These behaviors ultimately led me into a life of crime. At age fourteen shortly after my dad told me we were losing the house and I needed to find somewhere to live, I fell deeper into the street life. Eventually committing a felony drug offence, landing me in a Juvenile detention center for the first time. I was becoming a kid in and out of detention centers, kinship care, and foster homes moving from place to place with no hope for a bright future.

For the next few years, I struggled to get through probation. I had several probation violations with a two year sentence hanging over my head. At age 17 after removing my ankle monitor and running away from my foster home, I was committed to the Division of Youth Corrections (DYC). Through DYC, I was finally able to get the treatment and support that I needed. I was placed in a residential treatment center where I worked on many issues such as drugs, mental health, grief and loss, self-esteem and many other things. From treatment I finally gained the tools and resources that I needed to overcome my deepest darkest battles. It also helped to have a mentor that was there for me, believing in me and cheering for me every step of the way.

I successfully completed my treatment at the highest level, which was extremely hard to do. I went from a locked treatment facility to a less restrictive community treatment facility. Ready to prove that I was a changed person shortly after re- entering the community I received my high school diploma and found a job right away. I began to prepare for my independence working hard, saving money, and enrolling into college.

I successfully emancipated from the system at 19 and ever since, I have been destined to follow my dreams and to be a positive member of society. For several years after aging out I was actively involved in my community working on policy and legislation to improve systems of care. I spoke on youth panels, held seats on various boards such as; The National Policy Council for Foster Youth and Alumni, The Colorado Systems of Care steering committee, the Denver collaborative Partnership/ SB 94 board, the Denver Juvenile Court Best Practice Court Team, and the Clothes to Kids of Denver Community Advisory Council. I also had several opportunities to travel as a youth advocate and consultant on behalf of many organizations that provide services for children and youth.

In the summer of 2014 I got to be a Camp Counselor and Life Seminar facilitator at Camp to Belong Colorado. In 2015 I joined the Administrative team for camp as the volunteer coordinator and Life seminar facilitator. Camp to Belong Colorado is a national/international summer camp that once a year reunites siblings that are separated due to being in the Foster care system. In 2015 I became a Founding Board Member and helped to develop a non-profit organization that serves Foster youth called Elevating Connections INC where I now serve as the Program Manager, I was formerly a part of several different councils, boards, and committees. In 2016 I married my husband and had my first child. In 2020 Iaccomplished my goal of graduating with a Bachelor's degree from Metropolitan State University of Denver in Cross Systems Youth Services, a specialized degree I created.

If I had the Black Foster Youth Handbook available when I was in care it would have helped me during my teenage years to know that I wasn't alone. This would have been an amazing resource to build my self-esteem and help me get through my healing process. The Black Foster care Youth Handbook is an amazing resource and it highlights the journey of being a Black youth in care. I am so grateful for this amazing resource!

Learn more about Tamisha and Elevating Connections at
www.soulfulliberation.com/resources

ASCENSION
phase three

Chapter 7:

YOUR EXISTENCE MATTERS

Lesson 27:

LEARNING HOW TO LOVE YOUR BODY

- Am I hydrated today? How can I begin to make sure I am hydrated today and every day? Have I moved and stretched my body?
- Have I connected with someone I love today?
- Have I eaten at least three meals today?
- What kind of clothes makes me feel the most confident?
- What are my favorite features on my body? Why?
- What are my least favorite features about my body? Why?
- Has there ever been someone who said something negative about my body? Who and what did they say?

Lesson 28:

BLACKNESS IS PROFESSIONAL

#IAMSUCCESS QUESTIONS:

- How have I internalized these words?
- Why do I feel the need to hold on to these words as truth?

I AM SUCCESS WORKBOOK

Lesson 29:
EATING PLANT BASED IS NOT JUST A COOL FAD

- Did you know that each of your organs run on a cycle?
- What are Dr. Sebi and Queen Afua known for?
- Do you prioritize your physical well-being? Why or why not?
- How will you begin to prioritize your physical wellbeing?
- How is your current diet serving you in the long term?
- Do you care about having physical health? Why or why not?

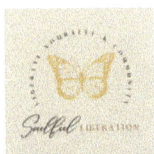

I AM SUCCESS WORKBOOK

Lesson 30:
PHYSICAL CONNECTION WITH SELF IS KEY

#IAMSUCCESS QUESTIONS:

- Do you pay attention to the signs and signals your body gives you?
- Do you drink alcohol or take drugs/medication to numb the pain instead of addressing the root cause? Why?
- What does your body posture say about you?
- Do you deal with skin issues? If so, what kind?
- What are you currently doing about aches, pains and skin breakouts?
- Which way have you connected with your body in the past?
- What do you want to learn in the future?
- How will you begin to connect with your body more?
- What is one thing you learned that you can share with a loved one today?

Lesson 31:
WATCH WHAT YOU CONSUME

#IAMSUCCESS QUESTIONS:

- What and who are you "paying attention to"?
- What experience and quality of people are you allowing into your energy? Why?
- Are you substituting overconsumption of media for happiness or love?
- Is there an emotional whole that you need to heal?
- What does mindful consumption look like to you?
- What do you feel you need to forgive yourself for?

I AM SUCCESS WORKBOOK

Lesson 32:
TRUE SELF LOVE TAKES WORK

- Do you have enough self-discipline to accomplish your goals?
- Are you procrastinating with what you believe you can achieve?
- Have you understood how to carry out your life's purpose?
- Are you making the most of your life?
- Do you have a planner? Are you setting goals for yourself with plans and deadlines?
- What is your definition of self-love?
- What is your definition of self-discipline?
- Who/What do you need to start following to see more of what you aspire to do and be?
- Who do you need to release to move forward?

Chapter Exercise
BUILDING YOUR CULTURALCONNECTION THROUGH ART

Write a letter to your body. And or/ different parts of your body that you recognize you are not necessarily happy with.

Repeat this process with each part of your body that you feel negative about. Make the time and be sure to honor the commitments you describe and promises to yourself.

Then, while holding your completed letter(s), stand in front of a full length mirror. Notice the thoughts and emotions that come up. You may decide to do this with or without clothes. My most effective results were when I was naked in front of the mirror and having to confront all things I hated about my face and body.

As I looked upon my facial features and full naked body, I felt a sense of disgust and annoyance. Different parts of my body even made me extremely sad due to memories of past sexual assault. All emotions and thoughts are normal and a part of the process. Stick with it, and you will find it easier and easier to do this will not be an overnight process to love your body.

Eventually, I learned how to accept my body for how it is and later was able to fall in love with my body as I have today.

EX. OF LETTER TO YOUR BODY:

Dear _____(ex. Curly, coily hair)

When I wear you natural, you make me feel _____
_____because_____
_____I hope to feel_____
_____ about you, curly, coily, hair, because that would mean
_____ _____.
The reason I currently feel this way about you curly, coily hair, is because _____
_____ _____. My
first memory feeling this way is _____
_____I was with _____
_____.
I apologize for treating you like _____
_____and will now work on loving you
wholeheartedly by._____
_____.I realize that no one is
coming to do this for me and I must make loving you a priority in order to stay on my path
toward success and leading a purposeful life unapologetically. Knowing this, I promise I will
begin because you are a part of to _____
_____ me and you are worth it. I am
worth it. I love you.

Signed,

Full Name

CEDRIC RILEY

I am dedicated to community leadership and success for myself and others. At the age of seven, my four siblings and I were placed in the Cuyahoga County Foster Care System due to parental neglect in Ohio. Placement in foster changed the course of my life. Though I was placed in different homes, I was able to adapt and learn the importance of relationship building.

I felt and knew that I needed to save my own life, and the key to it was a healthy relationship with myself. Feeling isolated from my family, I spent many nights traveling inside my own mind. Then something very special happened. My mind became a positive place where I could see my family members, friends and even myself in a future I imagined. I began to see this place in my dreams and the more I dreamt of it, the more majestic it became. After 8 1/2 years in the foster care system, I was adopted at 15 into a loving home in Cincinnati, Ohio where I experienced many scholastic and professional successes.

I shared my dream of becoming a motivational speaker with my mom and she helped me to achieve it. I gave my first speech to an international audience in 2007, expressing "Success is a Choice". Even though I was following my dream and big things were happening for me, my challenge of growing into an adult was not over. I had great ideas and aspirations but I had a character flaw that I needed to face. I was self-harming.

As an adult, I faced challenges including homelessness, and alcoholism which I was able to overcome through family support, intense discipline, community service and studying spiritual keys to growth like meditation and intentional dreaming. I came to believe there are three phases in life: Survival, Success and then Greatness. We must surpass the survival phase by understanding that we do not have to recycle the trauma that we experienced. In order to move beyond survival we must face our flaws. This is where respect for adults who are trying to help and an appreciation for relationship building come into play. I sat at the feet of many adults who were wiser than me and realized I could become the best version of myself. From there I was able to experience success. Success to me is growing out of old habits and ending the cycle of mistreating myself. This process took time, patience, and spiritual healing. I am now ready for greatness. I completed the NYC Marathon in the year 2017 and started my own tv show called 'America's Next Motivator!' where I interview other people who have been through foster care and life challenges. I am also married with children. I want to say to you, take charge of your life with all your might! Make it positive by respecting yourself and make life beautiful by allowing healthy relationships to take place. You are magnificent and you deserve to fulfill your dreams. You can make your life a dream come true! Survival, then Success, then Greatness!

Learn more about Cedric and America's Next Motivator at
www.soulfulliberation.com/resources

Chapter 8:

PROTECTING YOUR SPIRITUAL CONNECTION

Lesson 33:

SPIRITUALITY IS YOUR RELATIONSHIP WITH SELF

Lesson 34:
DON'T RUSH THE PROCESS

Lesson 35:
DIFFERENTIATING BETWEEN INTUITION AND SELF-SABOTAGE

- How can you begin to differentiate the two?
- Why is it important that you recognize self-sabotage when it shows up?
- When you begin to feel "off" what do you do, say or think about?
- It's important to ask yourself, " What am I feeling right now?
- Why am I feeling this way?"
- Where in your body are you feeling this?
- What are three words that can describe this feeling?
- Is there a lesson to be learned from this circumstance? You may have to dig deeper, it may not be surface level. What is the lesson?
- What do you need right now to alleviate this feeling?
- What small step can I take for mankind... lol... couldn't resist. But no, seriously. What small steps, today or this week can you take to meet your needs?

Lesson 36:
MAKE #SELFREFLECTION A DAILY HABIT

Lesson 37:
UNAPOLOGETICALLY EVOLVE

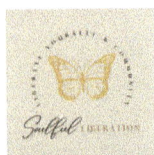

Chapter Exercise
CONNECTING WITH SELF

Go into a room that's quiet and close your eyes. You can have music or no music. Smile. Now, without moving your lips, say the words " I am safe."

If the world is just a physical plane with no substance, just a bunch of bad things happening with no way out... who just said that?

- Was it you?
- Was it God?
- Who is speaking when your mouth is closed?
- How can you hear the voice without it coming from outside of your body?
- How do you relax?
- What have you tried?
- What will you try to connect to yourself further?
- Have you heard of the 12 Universal Laws?
- What are the 12 Universal Laws?

JAI MCCLEAN

"For those currently experiencing foster care, I empathize with you. My heart beats for you. I want you to know there are men in women who may not have your story but have spent time in foster care like me, and are fighting for you and your rights! I want you to write and answer these questions down and this may take you a while to answer. In fact, this may take a lifetime to answer but, this will give you a different experience of your time in care. It's not too early to start making a plan for your life because only you are your best advocate! The questions you need to answer are the reason you exist.

The answer to these questions are the reason you breathe air in your lungs. The answer to these questions are the reason you will change the legacy of your family. The four questions are:

1. Who am I?
2. Where am I from?
3. What can I do?
4. Where am I going?

You are meaningful. You are enough. You are indeed a solution to the nations! Your life is more valuable than you understand and I need for you to take up that authority and walk in it! Discovering the answers to these questions as early on in your life will help you find your "why" in life that will lead you into your purpose!"

As a young girl, I understood that my family immigrated from another country and did not have access to some opportunities offered to United States citizens. Growing up in the projects of New York City, at the bright bold age of 5, I made a commitment to myself to help change the generational legacy of my family and create a better life for myself. I was 14 years old when I last saw my mother and bounced from home to home until I had the "opportunity" to enter foster care. Once given the option, I begrudgingly took it. At the age of 16, I found myself in a white Toyota Camry with the words 'Clark County Department of Family Services of Nevada' written on it. En-route to the nearest foster care agency in Las Vegas, Nevada, I devised a new plan to guide me to my intended destiny of one day becoming a physician. I decided I would use my privilege as a youth in foster care by any means necessary and have college paid for. Fast forward 4 years later, it was the summer of July 2017 and I'd just finished my junior year at the illustrious Hampton University! I'd traveled to Panama to perform a medical mission trip, completed 2 research projects and was given a provisional acceptance to Virginia Tech School of Medicine. I was well on my way to becoming a doctor right? Wrong!

The baggage and trauma associated with processing life as a foster youth weighed heavy on my back. I knew I was equipped with ambition, drive and determination, however I needed a savior and to save my own life before trying to save the life of another. I deserved that and so do you. That summer, I experienced a radical and personal encounter with God. I surrendered my life to Him and heard the words "I love you" from a God I always heard about but never knew personally. These three words peeled back years of abandonment and began a healing process that I desperately needed. Since then, I've been on a continuous journey of healing and in the words of Yvonne Orji being, "Bamboozled by Jesus," that has been ultimately, leading me to a path that was created just for me.

Learn more about Jai at www.soulfulliberation.com/resources

Chapter 9:

LEVEL UP, LEVEL UP, LEVEL UP

Lesson 38:

DON'T JUST HUSTLE, BUILD A LEGACY

#IAMSUCCESS QUESTIONS:

- What are the ways that I will begin to build a legacy for not only my life but the lives that will come after mine?
- Will it be financially, health wise or will I change the way I structure and maintain my relationships with people? Perhaps, you'll decide on all three.
- Are you already doing this in your own life?
- What is one way you will begin to build your legacy?
- What are you already doing to build a legacy?

Lesson 39:
YOU DO NOT HAVE TO REINVENT THE WHEEL

Lesson 40:
LOVING BLACKNESS IS ALSO LEADERSHIP

- What is the definition of a leader?
- Am I a leader?
- What is the problem you would like to begin to solve?
- Why is it important that it is solved?
- What can I do to support solving this issue?
- What business already exists that is actively working to solve this problem?
- Who can help me solve this problem?
- What resources am I lacking that could be in the way of me being able to solve this problem?

Lesson 40:
FAILURE IS NOT AN ENEMY

Lesson 42:

LIFE IS A SUM OF THE BELIEFS AND HABITS WE FIGHT FOR

Chapter Exercise
HABIT DEVELOPMENT

- What Ideas have you married?
- Are they causing you joy or grief?
- It's easy to fall off on habits that you are not used to having. I still fall off from maintaining
- proper eating routines.
- What are your current habits?
- What are some things you would like to start doing that you've been putting off because you don't think you can do it?

Talk with your adult supporter and see how you all can work together to get you another step closer to your goals.

Below is a Habit tracker that I created so that you can print it out at www.blackfostercareyouthhandbook.com and begin using it each and every month! Hang it somewhere you can see and make sure to let your adult supporters know so that they can help you stay accountable to your goals! Maybe they want to join you!

My Habits to Success

The Black Foster Youth Handbook

THIS MONTH OF _____, I PROMISE TO:

	MON	TUE	WED	THU	FRI	SAT	SUN
Habit:							
Habit:							
Habit:							
Habit:							

WHEN IT GETS TOUGH OR SCARY, I WILL DO IT ANYWAY!

Author's Note: If you are assigning chores to a young person, sit them down and explicitly share why having a sense of responsibility and giving examples of reciprocity in a relationship is important.

This will help the young person understand what is happening and why it is important for them to do this. Young people in foster care are often always told what to do by complete strangers. It's important to take time to explain why, even if you think they should know this already, they may not. How could they know certain basic concepts if no one taught them?

Then begin with one chore for the young person to begin implementing. After a while, you can create a list of chores that a young person can choose (2 or 3) as their responsibility on certain days and at certain times. They may not be consistent at first. Patience and repetition will be needed until they have something that will remind them to do it on their own.

Maybe type up a Responsibilities agreement between you and your young person. In this agreement, you list out the days and times you and the young person has agreed to complete

I AM SUCCESS WORKBOOK

chores. List the rewards for completing these chores and how often. Perhaps make some of the rewards being able to spend time together getting to know each other.

If you become frustrated, speak to your social worker, therapist and other seasoned foster parents that are not quick to remove their young person from their homes.

If you'd like to take it further, begin connecting with other like-minded foster/resource parents in your community and hold weekly or monthly meetings. This can be virtual or at a local coffee shop. Not just to talk about what is not going well with your new young person, but all the exciting new concepts, behaviors and ways that you are looking to support them with. Ask questions on how everyone can begin to support each other's young person. Maybe coordinate times for everyone and your young people to hang out

together. It's important to note that many young people in foster care self-isolate as a coping mechanism they learned throughout their lives.

Take time to get your young person out of the house and around other young people that are also on the path toward success. Begin scheduling to go on interactive personal development events to get your young person to think bigger than their current situation. Have space to just hang out and invite others who have young people over to join in the fun.

ERIC WARNER

"You are the strength that you need at any point in your life. This is to mean that even when you feel that you may not have enough strength to make it through a current challenge you are in that you never underestimate the amount of courage, strength and fortitude you have allotted to you. Never underestimate the amount of impactful change that you can create from the inner strength that comes only from facing the toughest challenges that confront our lives."

I (He/They pronouns) first entered care when I was 8 years old. Through a series of traumatic events and rehabilitation I was able to be reunified with my mother. This, unfortunately, would be an unsuccessful reunion and I would re-engage with the child welfare system at 11. While fighting with the turmoil of my youth and unwanted, forceful change it happened by chance I would have the opportunity to make a change in his life, which seemingly had spiraled out of control. This change came when my caseworker approached me about advocacy work with my local Youth Advisory Board (YAB). This would be the catalyst, that would launch the rest of my life in policy and reform change & advocacy. Whether it was losing the connections I had learned to cherish, or whether it was confronting the experiences (my perceived positive and negative) I have been able to tap into my resilience and inner strength to be able to move through his situation and come out on the "other side" scathed, but still strong and all the more wise. Though this might seem as a deterrence, my experience and sound knowledge relating to my varying placement settings, youth engagement, and advanced facilitation that I had learned since starting my advocacy career helped to propel me to conquer most challenges that I have seen set on my path. My personal connection to once being a recipient of services from child welfare allows me a continued and unique perspective when communicating with current and/or former youth in care regarding reformation and change implementation for states and differing nations. Utilizing, further, my skills in navigating the "aging-out" process and accessing services related to higher-education affords me a wide-set view for the changing and adverse needs related to the varying population that make up the foster care and related fields population.

After transitioning out of foster care, I found myself searching for a heightened purpose and familial connection that would come to me in a unique way. The family connection that has helped me become the person I am today with a refreshed gaze and enlightened emotional awareness. All to say that I am able to approach situations with a sense of knowing and connection to the topic engaged in. Further, one of my strongest lessons learned is that I create the family around me, even to the point of reintroducing biological relatives to the new meaning of family for me and what that would mean to re-engage with my life. Through this revolutionary time in my life I re-invigorated my passion for and engagement in higher education which resulted in seeking my college degree for my own personal enhancement and satisfaction. I have studied at an array of institutions but now attend courses from academia studying Criminal Justice in my pursuit for my B.A. In addition, I have been able to serve child welfare in varying roles within organizations on a local, state and federal level with each providing more opportunity to enhance my skills and passion for advancing child welfare work and reforming the current structure and ideology of systemic change and implementation. Along with these achievements, my most prized learnings have been of other capacities that ignite resiliency within youth and promote overall positive change in the lives of youth and maintaining permanence. Currently, consultation and collaborative implementation work will allow me the chance to commit my full areas of skill to bring about change needed to promote resilience, self-determination and establish/maintain sufficiency of services and standards for children and young adults in care. Although I may possess these skills it is my intention to share these learning with those who share similar passions and interests for change and reformation among child welfare!

Learn more about Eric at www.soulfulliberation.com/resources

LIBERATION

phase four

Chapter 10:

YOUR VOICE MATTERS

Lesson 43:

YOUR STORY IS NOTHING TO BE ASHAMED OF

Lesson 44:
MIND YOUR OWN BUSINESS BEFORE SPEAKING ON OTHERS

Instead of explaining something off or trying to turn the situation back around on another person, it may serve better value to acknowledge what is being said and see how we can face the reality, without covering it up of the words or action we have used. Do not disown it or change the subject. Do not flip the script. Before you respond, listen and accept what is being said.

- When someone tells you that you've done something to hurt their feelings or betray their trust, how do you react?
- Do you compassionately try to understand why you said or did what was done?
- Do you recognize the person or people involved and convey a clear knowing and understanding of the damage done?
- Do you sincerely apologize and try to find ways on how you can reconcile with the person or people who were affected?
- Do you commit to changed behavior after going through the previous questions

Lesson 45:
I CAN SAY NO TO AN "OPPORTUNITY"

SHARE YOUR STORY

> "Get in good trouble, necessary trouble."
>
> CONGRESSMAN JOHN LEWIS

I met Congressman John Lewis in 2017 with a leading organization in child welfare. He was one of the leading social activists for the well-known sit in movement. He has been an incredible African-American leader and among those who laid their entire lives on the line to create the necessary changes for people of color to gain access to the basic necessities of life, have a voice and be treated like human beings.

I encourage you to watch his film, Good Trouble.
Connect with other young people currently experiencing or have experienced foster care through Facebook groups and in your local organizations. A simple google search may be all you need to help you find your next friend!

Look for opportunities to speak out about the causes that matter most to you.

Think about how you would like to share your story. There are many different types of advocacy and many ways you can get involved in your community. Figure out which ones work best for you.

It is also important to keep in mind that you and your story are valuable. Just because you believe it will help others to share it, doesn't mean you need to do it at the expense of your own mental, physical or emotional health.

Think to yourself, is the return of the investment for me sharing your story worth it?

If you believe it is, then move forward with it. Be cautious, and know your worth.

ALIYAH ZEIEN

"Everyday we can all work to be the caring and loving adults we needed as children. Everything you need to succeed is already within you, as greatness is in us all. Everything I have now, I used to pray and dream about. We all have the potential to become a living testament of what can happen when you don't give up. We have survived a lifetime of tragedies, but through that there is triumph, and through our pain there is power. We can all exceed the expectations that have been placed on us. "

I am 25 years old now. Everything I have achieved used to literally be only a dream. Something I would hope and wish could happen. I am the oldest of five siblings. During my childhood years I endured physical, emotional, and sexual abuse. The abuse really began to escalate after I had to live with my mother full time at the age of 8, following my grandmother passing away. From birth until around 7/8 my grandmother was my primary caregiver, until she died from Lung Cancer. I come from a dysfunctional and toxic family that has a history of drug use, poverty, and incarceration. I thought my story was already written for me. But that's the thing about stories, we always have the power to write the next chapter.

Due to everything I survived as a child, I committed myself to breaking the generational curses that had plagued my family. I entered the foster care system at age 13, after years of crying for help. I had three total placements. In my second placement, I finally settled down, and became comfortable. I was engaged in sports, making good grades and had a few reliable friends.

I was bonded with my caregivers and involved in church. Unfortunately I wasn't aware of my foster mothers health conditions. In May 2011 I held her hand as she clenched, gasped for air and took her last breath. She died in front of me.
A part of me changed that day.

I had witnessed death, abuse, and tragedy. After that I had yet another move. I entered my third and final placement. During that time, instead of really healing from my grief, I threw myself into busy work. While I did become bonded with that family, there were just certain walls I built that I couldn't really take down. I became apart of the track team, did community service activities, and constantly poured into my school work. I excelled at everything because when I was growing up it was made clear to me education would be one of the only ways "out." I graduated St. Helena high school at age 17. From there I was accepted into Southeastern Louisiana University. While in college I began doing extensive advocacy work and obtained my first direct service position as a Peer Support Specialist with the Louisiana independent living programs. I obtained a bachelors in social work in 2017.

Two days before graduation I sat in my car and broke down in tears. I had already exceeded well above what I ever expected to achieve. I prayed and whispered "grandma we made it." After graduation I went on to accept a position at DCFS as a Child Welfare Specialist. After completing my year work contract, I resigned and refocused on my advocacy work. I rejoined the Life Skills Team as a Life Skills Specialist, and I completed the FYI legislative internship at the LA Capitol. I have been an NFYI shadow day intern. In Louisiana I have worked diligently with our state youth advisory board to pass the Extended foster care legislation and write the first foster youth bill of rights. Last year I opened my own bakery business which has truly flourished. I'm a LSU MSW intern. With the help and support of my connective network, I have used everything that was meant to break me to build me. This year I became the Vice President of the Louisiana State Youth Advisory Board and the State Youth Ambassador. I am the first former foster youth to hold this position. I am honored with everything God has blessed me with. I say all this to say that people used to think I would turn out to be a drug addict, a failure, etc, however I am now a walking testimony. I am literally fueled to make a difference because of everything I went through. And that's what we can all do.

Learn more about Aliyah at www.soulfulliberation.com/resources

Chapter 11

CULTIVATING AND SUSTAINING INNER PEACE

Lesson 46:

KNOW YOUR WORTH

Lesson 47:
WE NEED TO RELAX MORE

- What kind of conversations are you having?
- Are they mostly enjoyable and life giving or negative and gossiping?
- If you find yourself in a verbal altercation, challenge yourself to ask questions like: "Why did they do that?" and Do I need to respond to this person?

- How can I respond in a way that will deescalate the situation while getting my point across?" "What will help solve this issue- silence, a response, giving space?"
- Before engaging in any activity (bad or good) ask yourself, what is my goal? What am I trying to accomplish with participating in this behavior/ event?
- What are the possible consequences to this word choice/ action?
- Is it really worth it right now and in the long run?
- Will this action bring me forward or drag me toward the past?

Lesson 48:
INCREASING YOUR FINANCIAL EDUCATION

- What is money's purpose?
- What is the purpose of giving money in my life?
- What is my yearly/monthly/weekly/daily income goal?
- How do I begin to save it?
- How much do I want to save by the end of the next 3 months? 6 months? A year?
- Where will I house and invest my money? What options are available?
- How can I utilize it as a tool to create the life I desire?
- How will I begin to use money to support others in my community?
- What causes am I interested in supporting?
- What is the purpose of credit?
- What skills am I missing in order to level up?

Lesson 49:
LEARNING SELF-DEFENSE

Lesson 50:
HOLISTIC HEALTH IS WEALTH

Chapter Exercise
PRIORITIZE RELAXING AND PROTECTING YOUR PEACE

Begin to prioritize relaxing and protecting your peace into your schedule. Here is a Soul Care Checklist to help you check in each week. If you are not feeling well, see if you have done any of these. You may find that you have not and may need to do one or more of these tasks on your schedule! Consider even taking a 7 day social media or food fast. Take care of your peace, family. We cannot give from an empty cup.

SOUL CARE
CHECKLIST

The Black Foster Youth Handbook by Ángela Quijada-Banks

- Taking time to deep breathe
- Staying Hydrated
- Getting good amount of rest
- Did atleast ONE exciting thing
- Using essential oils
- Took a spiritual bath
- Got a massage
- Entertained my creativity
- Laughed every day
- Moisturized my skin
- Not entertaining drama
- Beautified my space
- Eating a well-balanced meal
- Watched feel-good content
- Hanging out with amazing ppl
- Monitored my social media intake
- Retail therapy
- Participating in physical activity
- Meditating regularly
- Plans for a vacay
- Rooting in purpose
- Released negativity
- Spent time in nature
- Did something that wasn't comfortable

NOTES

CHRISTINA PARKER

"Dear foster youth, this world may not see us, and unfortunately, that is a lot of our realities. But I'm here to tell you that it doesn't matter what they say you can't do, who you will or will not be. Hold onto your dreams and chase them because you are capable of anything you put your mind to. There isn't a statistic that can predict what you will accomplish and how far you will go.

We shouldn't have to fight but giving up should never be our option no matter how difficult it may be. Ask yourself " who am I, and who do I want to be?" and go through life doing everything to reach that. Utilize what you have around you to grow inspiration and motivation. Don't stop because you don't see the immediate outcome or you experience barriers.

The journey is never easy but I'm confident that you will become something magnificent. You are important, intelligent, and more than capable.

We are really out here beating all of the odds, But our book will never be complete until yours is added."

I was more than a tulip or a daisy, destined to grow no matter how many times they buried me! I was destined to grow no matter how many times they poisoned my soil and pouredconcrete over me! I was going to grow with or without people pouring into me! They called it resiliency, hidden behind their attempt to stifle my growth, but to their surprise, I still grow.

I spent 18-years in the foster care system through kinship placement. Being a black foster child meant that my standards and outcomes were predicted and lowered for me. I was placed in special education because my school district wouldn't invest time into addressing my needs and despite not having a learning disability, I stayed in special education until the last semester of my senior year in high school. I was told that I could not go to college by counselors, teachers, and other professionals. My entire life I faced limitations and judgment because of experiences I had no control over and instead of people encouraging me, they enabled me, refused to see me, and support me. I became tired of people limiting what I was capable of accomplishing and I knew if I didn't fight I'd become another statistic. I realized that no one had to see me because I saw who I was and most importantly who I could be. I went through a rigorous process but eventually exited special education, fought my school on taking classes for college, sacrificed time to get support from after-school programs, and started to excel academically. I went from a student who could barely get a 2.0 to now making the honor roll in college. I became a mentor, a person that has changed legislation and policy to support others in the foster care system, and developed a college support platform for thousands of students eager to go to college. I became everything they couldn't imagine.

Learn more about Christina at www.soulfulliberation.com/resources

Chapter 12:

BE IN A CONSTANT STATE OF TRANSFORMATION

Lesson 51:

KNOWING YOUR PURPOSE IS LIFE CHANGING

Lesson 52:
MY ONLY COMPETITION IS WITH MY PAST SELF

Lesson 53:
ALCHEMIZING PAIN

Lesson 54:
THERE IS A CHAIN OF COMMAND IN FOSTER CARE

#IAMSUCCESS QUESTIONS:

- How do you view family?
- Are you open to having support from the supportive adults around you?
- On a scale of 1-10, how safe do you feel in the home?
- What could be done to make you feel more safe?
- Who are the top three people that you trust right now?
- Are you willing to grow your list of trustworthy people? Why or why not?
- Are you a trustworthy person?
- What is the chain of command in my case plan?
- Who are people you can talk to when you feel down or frustrated about something?

Lesson 55:

AGING OUT OF FOSTER CARE DOESN'T HAVE TO BE LONELY

ABOUT
THE AUTHOR

Angela Quijada Banks

Ángela Quijada-Banks is an NAACP Image Awards Nominated, American author of the best-selling book, The Black Foster Youth Handbook, and a holistic wellness coach. She is the Founder of Soulful Liberation which started as a podcast to support young people with trauma to navigate their healing journey during the pandemic and has expanded into a movement where she aims to support the journey of self exploration, healing and transformation in our communities!

As a transformational speaker and artist, she has impacted thousands with her message to alchemize your pain to purpose and power.

Ángela is a scholar at Legacy Holistic Health Institute studying Holistic Health and wellness through natural indigenous plant-based modalities. She is a wife to an incredible husband and a cat mom to two crazy kittens. Ángela aims to aid in revolutionary changes in the areas of holistic health, economic injustices, child-welfare disparities, cultural awareness and identity within low-wealth communities of color both on a micro and macro level.

Connect with Ángela at www.angelaquijadabanks.com

WORK WITH US

For workshops, training and coaching visit **www.soulfulliberation.com**

Book orders for Black Foster Youth Handbook and I Am Success Workbook visit
www.blackfostercareyouthhandbook.com

Book Ángela or learn more visit **www.angelaquijadabanks.com**

To connect with us, Email **info@soulfulliberation.com**

Thank you !!

Thank you for joining me on this journey toward Soulful Liberation!

I cannot wait to hear from you!

★★★★★

Wanna help spread the word about this book?

1. Be sure to leave an honest review on Amazon!

2. Tell someone about it!

3. Encourage your local foster care organization to purchase bulk copies.

www.ingramcontent.com/pod-product-compliance
Lightning Source LLC
Chambersburg PA
CBHW040248290326

41929CB00057B/3477